# BOATS AND SHIPS

SUSAN HARRIS

**An Easy-Read Fact Book**

Franklin Watts
New York l London l 1979

Illustrated by Phillip Biffen, Ken Fleming,
Elaine Lee, Michael Toohig and E. Smart.

Library of Congress Cataloging in Publication Data

Harris, Susan.
  Boats and ships.

  (An Easy-read fact book)
  Includes index.
  SUMMARY: Introduces various types of ships and boats and highlights their history and uses.
  1. Ships—History—Juvenile literature. 2. Boats and boating—History—Juvenile literature.
  [1. Ship—History. 2. Boats and boating—History]
  I. Biffen, Phillip. II. Title.
  VM150.H33         387.2              78-11344
  ISBN 0-531-02270-6

All rights reserved
Printed in the United Kingdom
6  5  4  3  2  1

## R.L. 2.8 Spache Revised Formula

# BOATS AND SHIPS

**The Royal Yacht** *Britannia* **entering Sydney Harbor**

Boats are fun.

This is true whether they are toy boats or large ships.

But they are more than fun. Boats and ships are important, too.

They carry people from one country to another.

They move **cargo** down rivers and across oceans.

And during a war, they can move soldiers and guns from one place to another.

Boats are made out of almost anything that will float.

**Rafts** were some of the earliest boats. They are made by tying pieces of wood together.

American explorers used rafts to explore rivers.

People who lived on islands in the Pacific Ocean sailed large rafts on the sea.

An explorer named Thor Heyerdahl (HI-er-doll) built a raft called the *Kon-Tiki.* He sailed it across the Pacific Ocean in 1947.

By doing this, he proved something important. He proved that the first Pacific Islanders might have come by raft from South America.

Another common boat is the **dugout canoe** (ka-NU). This canoe is made by digging out a tree trunk. The ends are then shaped.

The world's largest canoe is a dugout canoe. It was built by the natives of New Zealand. It is 117 feet (35 m) long and can carry 70 people.

**Maori dugout canoes**

Today, there are two common types of canoes.

One kind is open all along its length. In the past, North American Indians carved them from trees. They used them to fish and to travel along rivers and streams. Today, they are used mainly for pleasure.

All canoes are lightweight. They make little noise as they move through the water.

**Canoeing in an open canoe**

Kayaking with a double-bladed paddle

Another type of canoe is called a **kayak** (KI-yak). Kayaks are completely covered, except for the **cockpit**. This is the hole where the paddler sits.

The paddler steers the kayak with one double-bladed paddle.

Eskimos made some of the first kayaks. They used wood and animal skins. Today, most kayaks are made from fiber glass.

Rowing was a popular pastime in the 1890s.

**Rowboats** are popular for use on lakes and ponds.

They are usually wider and heavier than canoes or kayaks. They don't tip over as easily, either.

Years ago, rowboats had **rudders** for steering.

Today, the person rowing can steer by using the two oars. He or she just pulls harder on one oar than on the other.

Some people race rowboats.

Racing boats called **shells** are built for speed. They are lightweight and narrow. They can move through the water easily and quickly.

Some shells carry only one racer. Others can carry as many as eight.

Teams compete against each other at races called **regattas** (re-GA-tas).

A racing shell and its crew

Moving a boat with paddles or oars can be very tiring.

Long ago, people discovered that wind could move a boat if the boat had **sails**.

For thousands of years, sailing was the main way to travel on water. Today, however, sailing is done mostly for fun and sport.

Sailing dinghy

Racing yachts, with colorful sails set

Sailing regatta

The most popular kind of sailboat is called a **sloop**. It has two sails. The big sail is called the **mainsail**. The smaller sail is called the **foresail** or **jib**.

The boat is steered by moving the mainsail and the rudder.

The **keel** keeps the boat from tipping over.

A sailboat can sail in any direction. It doesn't matter which way the wind is blowing.

But to sail directly into the wind, it has to **tack**. This means it moves in a zigzag path.

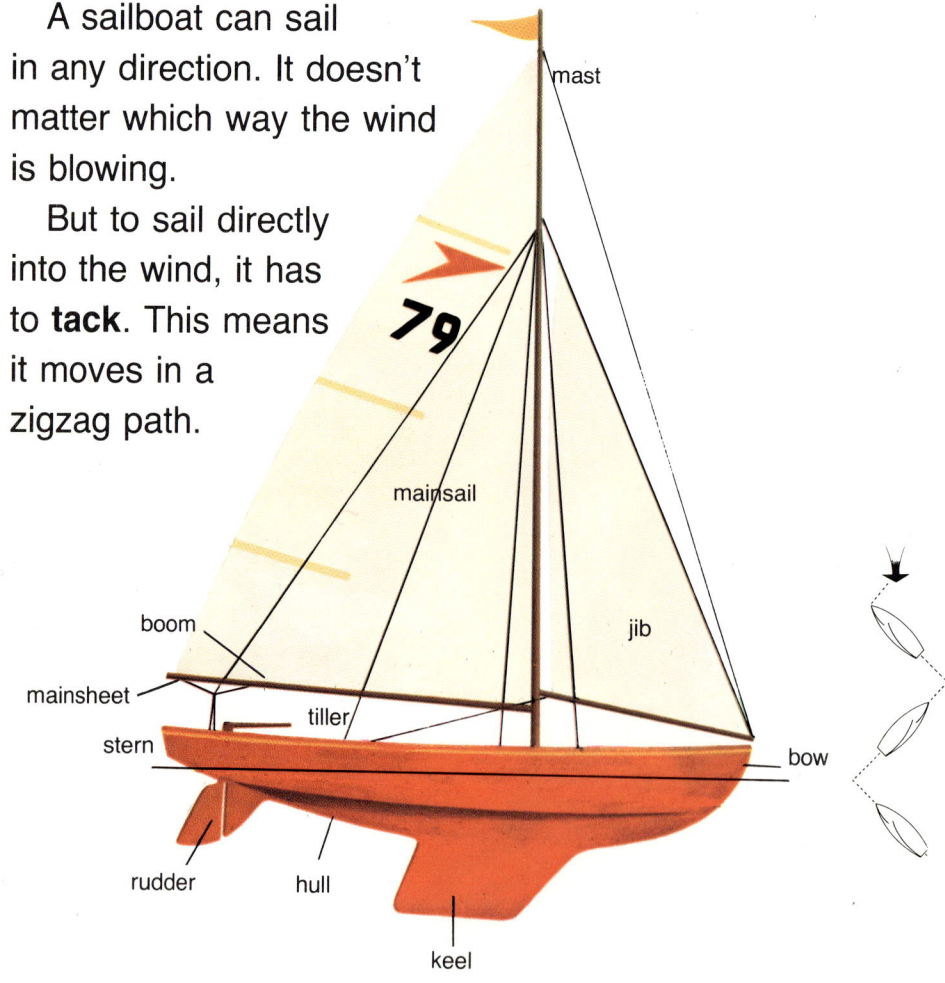

14

Sloops are only one kind of sailboat. Some other, larger sailboats are called **cutters, ketches, yawls,** and **schooners**.

Each type of boat is rigged differently. **Rigging** means the number and placement of masts and sails.

**Cutter**—a one-masted boat with a mainsail, two foresails, and a bowsprit.

**Ketch**—a two-masted boat with two foresails and a sail on the rear (mizzen) mast. The mizzen mast is shorter than the mainmast. A yawl is similar, but its mizzen mast is much further back.

**Schooner**—a two- or three-masted boat. The forward mast is shorter than or the same size as the mainmast.

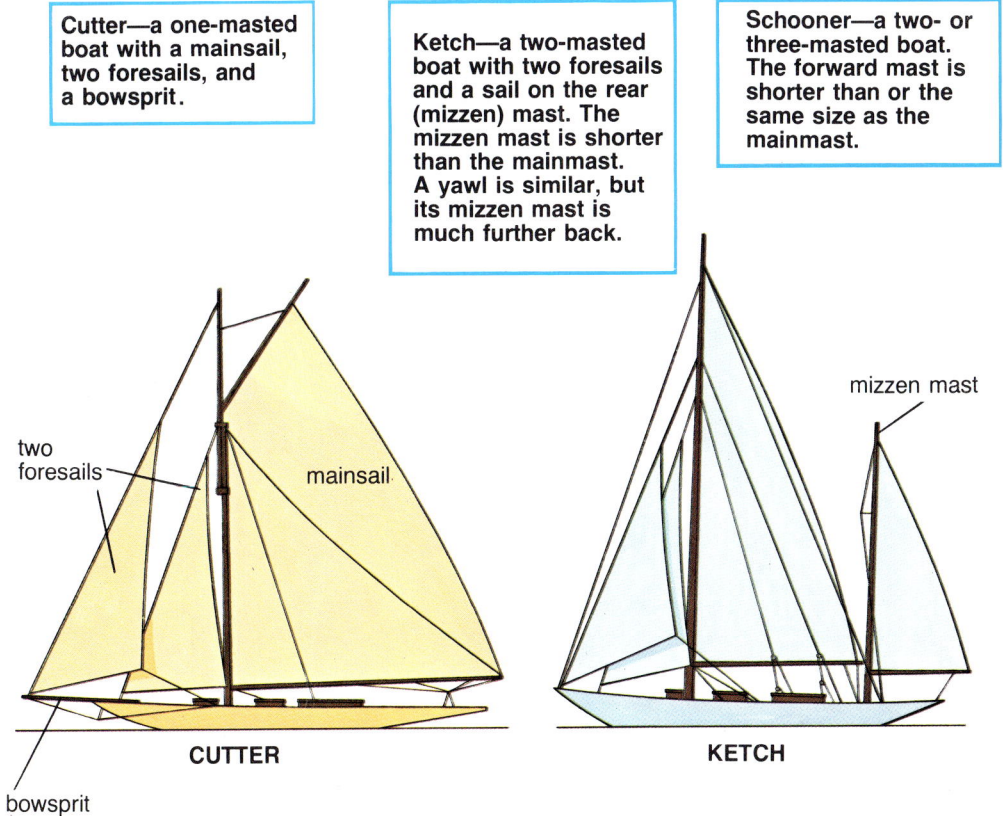

The finest sailing ships were called **clippers**. They were built in the early 1800s.

Some carried tea from China to Europe and North America.

Others carried supplies to San Francisco during the California gold rush.

Clippers had huge sails and narrow ends. They could sail at great speeds.

But sailing ships were important only until the **steamship** was developed.

Steamships were faster and easier to run than sailing ships.

They could also sail even when there was no wind.

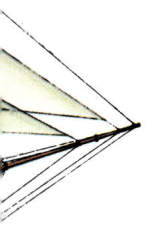

Today, full-rigged ships are used to train sailors and for racing in regattas.

17

**Chinese junk**

Some interesting sailboats can be found today in the Middle and Far East.

Chinese **junks** are made to sail both rivers and oceans. They have flat bottoms. Often, they are used as houseboats.

With their huge triangular sails, Arab **dhows** (daws) are very fast. Long ago, they were used by pirates. Today, Arabs use them for fishing.

The galley (kitchen) and shower of a cruiser

Today, many larger sailing boats have **cabins**.

People can eat and sleep in them during a long trip. They have beds (called **berths**) and toilets (called **heads**). They even have kitchens (called **galleys**).

Large sailboats usually have an engine as well as sails. This way they can move even when there is no wind.

Many boats, of course, have no sails. They use engines to move them through the water.

The engine is connected to a **propeller**. This is at the stern (the back of the boat).

The propeller spins very fast. As it does, it pushes the boat forward.

**Motorboat**

**Catamaran**

    The **hull** of a boat is the part that sits in the water. Most boats have only one hull. But some have two. Some even have three.

    A boat with two hulls is called a **catamaran** (cad-a-ma-RAN). A boat with three hulls is called a **trimaran** (TRI-ma-ran).

    Sailing catamarans have tall sails. They can move very fast.

One of the fastest kinds of boat is the **hydrofoil** (HI-dro-foil).

It has curved metal "wings" called **foils**. These are attached to the hull.

As the boat moves faster, the hull lifts out of the water. The boat then sails on the foils.

The small foils make less **drag** (resistance) in the water than large hulls. This is why hydrofoils can move so fast.

**Hydrofoil**

Among the smaller boats that sail the sea are **fishing boats**.

They are strong and sturdy boats. They have to sail in even the roughest weather.

The **drifter** is a common fishing boat. It catches fish in long drift nets. These are nets that hang in the water like a wall.

Fish become trapped as they swim into the net.

◀ Drifter

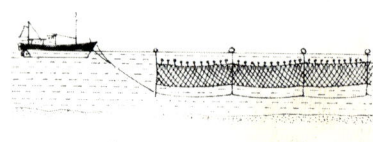

▲ Drifter with drift net

The **trawler** is another kind of fishing boat. It too uses a net.

The net is dragged behind the boat as the boat moves through the water.

It can be dragged along the bottom of the sea. Or it can be dragged higher up in the water.

The net full of fish is then pulled in.

◀ Trawler

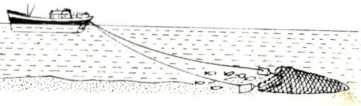

Trawler with trawl net

It's hard to believe that these tiny **tugboats** can pull this huge ship. But they can. In fact, it's their job.
Tugboats guide larger ships into ports and harbors.

**Dredgers** (DRE-jers) can also be seen in harbors. Their job is to dig out mud and sand from the harbor bottom. This makes it possible for large ships to pass through.

**Grab dredger**

**Bucket dredger**

Before airplanes became so popular, most people crossed the oceans on **passenger liners**.

These huge ships could carry hundreds of people. They had swimming pools and restaurants. Some even had libraries and theatres.

But today most people fly long distances. For this reason there are only a few passenger liners left.

Passenger liners are made so that they do not roll in rough seas. They are fitted with moving fins that stick out from the sides of the hull. These keep the ship from tilting to one side or another.

High above the **cabins** (private rooms) is the ship's **bridge**. It is from here that the captain controls and steers the ship.

The captain uses **navigation** (na-vi-GA-shun) **equipment**. With this, he always knows exactly where the ship is.

Below the bridge are rows of lifeboats. They are used only in case of an emergency.

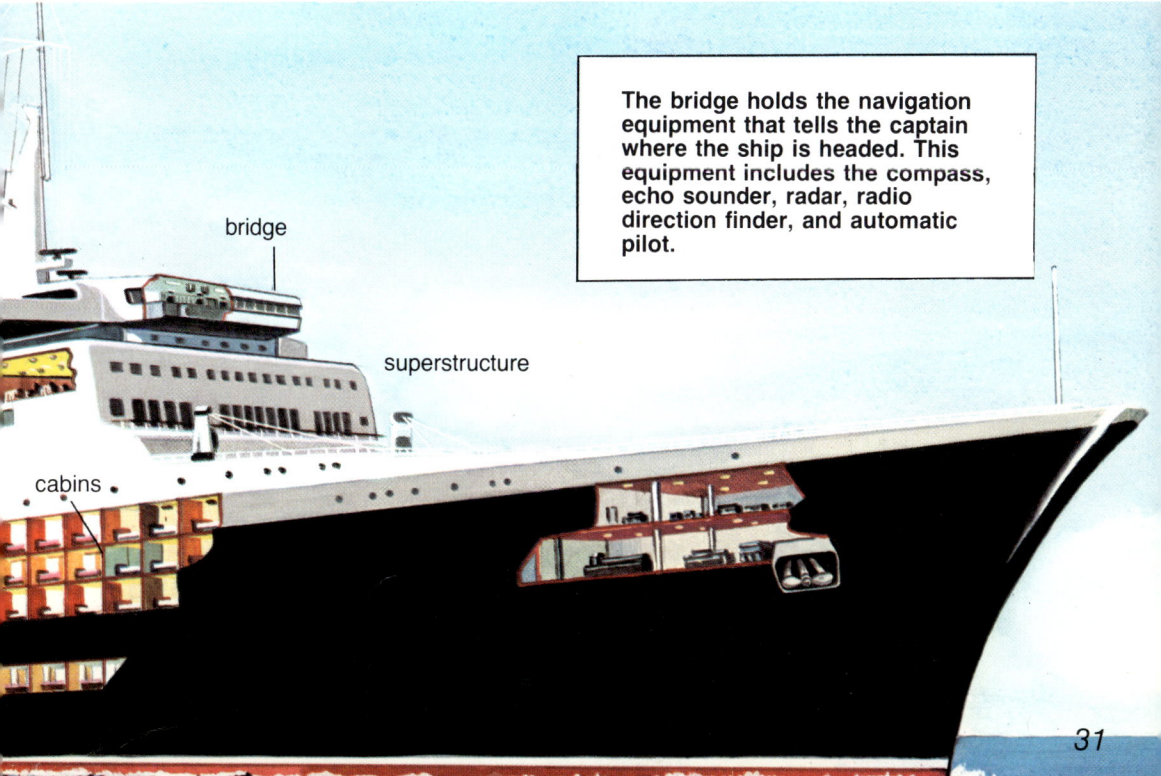

**The bridge holds the navigation equipment that tells the captain where the ship is headed. This equipment includes the compass, echo sounder, radar, radio direction finder, and automatic pilot.**

bridge

superstructure

cabins

**Freighter in port next to storage warehouses**

derrick

cargohold

Passenger liners may be more exciting than **cargo ships**. But they are not as important today. Cargo ships, or **freighters** (FRA-ters), cross the oceans carrying goods from one country to another.

There are many kinds of freighters. They are all made for different kinds of cargo.

Some may carry meat, tea, or sugar. Others carry coal, wood, or oil.

Freighters can usually be recognized by their many **derricks**. These are poles used to swing cargo onto and off the ship.

Ships load and unload their cargo at **ports**.

When the cargo is unloaded, it is sometimes stored in warehouses.

At many ports, the rise and fall of the **tide** would make loading and unloading very difficult. So these ports have **docks**.

A dock is an area of water that can be cut off from the sea. This is done with watertight gates. When the gates are closed, the water level doesn't change.

Sometimes the bottom of a ship needs to be repaired. Then it goes into **dry dock**.

**Ship unloading cargo by means of overhead cranes**

**Ship in dry dock**

Container port

Dry docks are areas where the water can be pumped out. Then the ship's bottom can be painted or repaired.

Some ports have special machines to handle **containers**.

Containers are huge boxes that can hold all kinds of cargo.

The largest ships are **oil tankers**. They carry the oil that is made into gasoline and other fuels.

Some tankers are 1,312 feet (400 m) long and 207 feet (63 m) across. They carry more than 454,545 tons (500,000 tonnes) of oil.

Even though tankers are so big, they need only a small crew. They are run mostly by **automatic equipment**.

Oil tankers can be recognized by their long, low decks.

▲ Lightships by night and day ▲

**Lightships** can also be easily recognized.

These are actually floating lighthouses. They are anchored near undersea wrecks and other dangers to ships.

37

**Ferry**

Another useful kind of cargo boat is the **ferry**. Ferries carry people, cars, and trucks for short distances.

They are sturdy craft with very powerful engines. They can work in very rough seas.

Some ferry routes are not worked by ships, but by **hovercraft** (HOV-er-kraft).

Hovercraft don't sail through or on the water. Instead, they skim above the waves on a layer of air.

They are pushed by air propellers. They can go as fast as 17 knots (20 miles [32 km] per hour).

**Hovercraft**

Ships have always played an important part in wars.

Most powerful nations have large **fleets** (groups of ships).

Years ago, the most important warships were **battleships**. They had thick armor and huge guns. They were slow and heavy.

Today, fleets are made up of lighter, faster warships, such as **destroyers** or **frigates** (FRIG-its).

**Aircraft carrier**

**Frigate**

Modern warships have all kinds of **electronic equipment**.

With it, they can find and destroy enemy ships and aircraft.

Huge **aircraft carriers** carry airplanes on their long, flat decks. Planes take off from and land on these ships. Their decks are used as floating runways.

**Submarines** are ships that can stay under water safely for some time.

Some are powered by electric motors and batteries. They have to come to the surface often.

Some new submarines, however, run on **nuclear** (NU-kle-ar) **power**. These can stay under water for months at a time.

**Left: controls inside a submarine
Far left and above: submarines**

**The building dock, where the hull is made**

**Miles of piping on a modern supertanker**

Until the 1800s, most ships were made of wood. Then iron and, finally, steel were used.

Today, nearly all big ships are built with steel hulls. The hull is built by joining together large steel **plates**.

All large ships are built with a lot of metal. A modern oil tanker may contain as much as 30 miles (48 km) of metal pipes alone.

When the hull is finished, the ship is given a name. Then it is **launched**, or placed into the water.

But it is not ready to sail yet.

It must first go to a **fitting-out yard**. Here it has its machinery put in place.

Soon after that, the ship is ready to sail.

**A carrier just after launching**

# Famous Ships of the Past

Egyptian galley

Greek warship

Viking longship

Cargo ship of the Middle Ages

Caravel, 1400s

Spanish Galleon, 1500s

Paddle Wheel Steamship, 1850s

*Lusitania*, 1900s

Clipper, 1850

47

# Index

Aircraft carriers, 40, 41
Automatic equipment, on tankers, 36

Battleships, 40
Berth, 20
Bridge, ship's, 31
*Britannia* (royal yacht), 2

Cabin, ship's, 31
Canoes, 7–9
Caravel, 47
Cargo, 5
Cargo ships (freighters), 33–35
Catamaran, 22
Clipper ships, 16–17, 47
Construction of boats and ships, 6, 44
Containers, and cargo ships, 34, 35
Cutter, 15

Derricks, on cargo ships, 33, 34
Destroyers, 40
Dhow, Arab, 18, 19
Docks, and cargo ships, 34
Dredger, 27, 29
Drifter, 24
Dry docks, 34–35
Dugout canoe, 7

Electronic equipment, and warships, 41
Eskimos, and kayaks, 9

Ferries, 38
Fishing, 18
Fishing boats, 18, 24–26

Fitting-out yard, 45
Fleets, warship, 40
Foil, 23
Freighters (cargo ships), 32, 33, 35
Frigates, 40, 41

Galley, 20

Head, 20
Heyerdahl, Thor, 7
Hovercraft, 39
Hull, 22
Hydrofoil, 23

Indians, and canoes, 8

Jib (sail), 14
Junk, Chinese, 18

Kayak, 9
Keel, 14
Ketch, 15
*Kon-Tiki* (raft), 7

Launching, of ships, 45
Lifeboats, 31
Lightships, 37
*Lusitania*, 47

Navigation equipment, 31
Nets, fishing, 24, 26
Nuclear power, and submarines, 42

Oars, for rowboats, 10

Paddles, for canoes, 9
Paddlewheeler, 47

Passenger liners, 30–33
Pirates, 18
Ports, and cargo ships, 34, 35
Propellers, on engines, 21

Rafts, 6–7
Regattas, 10, 11
Rowboats, 10–11
Rudder, 10, 14

Sailboats, 14–20
  cabins in, 20
  rigging of, 15
Sailing, 12, 14
Sails, types of, 14
Schooner, 15
Sloop, 14
Spanish galleon, 47
Steamships, 17
Steel, in shipbuilding, 44
Submarines, 42

Tacking, 14
Tankers, oil, 36
Tides, and loading ships, 31
Trawler, 26
Trimaran, 22
Tugboats, 28

Viking longship, 46

Warships, 40–42
Wind, and sailboats, 12, 14
Wood, in shipbuilding, 44

Yawl, 15

Thanks are due to the following for kind permission to reproduce photographs:

Christopher Blackwell; Central Office of Information; Colvic Craft Limited; Harland and Wolff Limited; Hoverlloyd Limited; Ministry of Defence; New Zealand High Commission; P. & O. Group Limited; Port of London Authority; Roger Smith; Thames Marine Limited; Trinity House Lighthouse Service; United States Naval Forces, Europe; United States Tourist Office; John Watney; Westminster Dredging Group Limited; White Fish Authority.